~A BINGO BOOK~

Grammar and Usage Bingo Book

COMPLETE BINGO GAME IN A BOOK

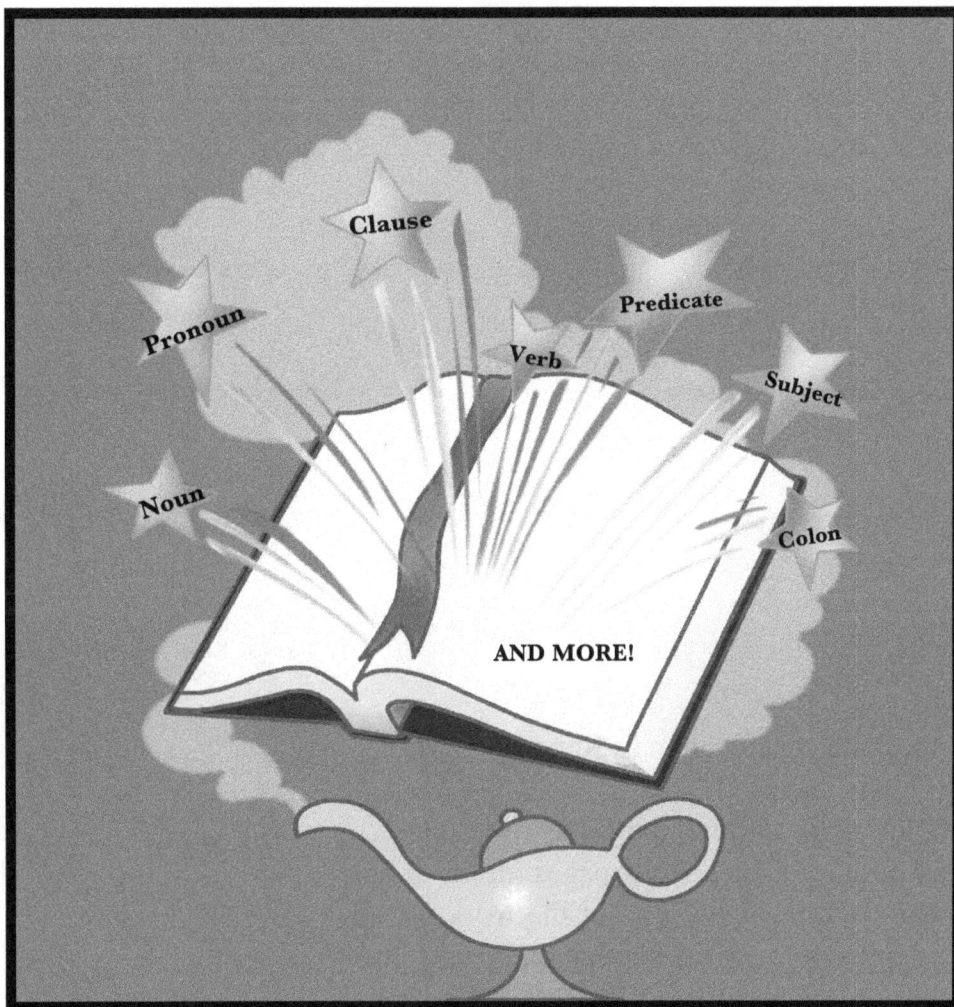

Clause

Predicate

Pronoun

Verb

Subject

Noun

Colon

AND MORE!

Written By Rebecca Stark
Educational Books 'n' Bingo

TITLE: Grammar and Usage Bingo
AUTHOR: Rebecca Stark

ISBN 978-0-87386-485-5

Educational Books 'n' Bingo

Printed in the U.S.A.

GRAMMAR & USAGE BINGO DIRECTIONS

INCLUDED:

List of Terms

Templates for Additional Terms and Clues

2 Clues per Term

30 Unique Bingo Cards

Markers

1. **Either cut apart the book or make copies of ALL the sheets. You might want to make an extra copy of the clue sheets to use for introduction and review. Keep the sheets in an envelope for easy reuse.**

2. Cut apart the call cards with terms and clues.

3. Pass out one bingo card per student. There are enough for a class of 30.

4. Pass out markers. You may cut apart the markers included in this book or use any other small items of your choice.

5. Decide whether or not you will require the entire card to be filled. Requiring the entire card to be filled provides a better review. However, if you have a short time to fill, you may prefer to have them do the just the border or some other format. Tell the class before you begin what is required.

6. There are 50 terms. Read the list before you begin. If there are any terms that have not been covered in class, you may want to read to the students the term and clues before you begin.

7. There is a blank space in the middle of each card. You can instruct the students to use it as a free space or you can write in answers to cover terms not included. Of course, in this case you would create your own clues. (Templates provided.)

8. Shuffle the cards and place them in a pile. Two or three clues are provided for each term. If you plan to play the game with the same group more than once, you might want to choose a different clue for each game. If not, you may choose to use more than one clue.

9. Be sure to keep the cards you have used for the present game in a separate pile. When a student calls, "Bingo," he or she will have to verify that the correct answers are on his or her card AND that the markers were placed in response to the proper questions. Pull out the cards that are on the student's card keeping them in the order they were used in the game. Read each clue as it was given and ask the student to identify the correct answer from his or her card.

10. If the student has the correct answers on the card AND has shown that they were marked in response to the *correct questions,* then that student is the winner and the game is over. If the student does not have the correct answers on the card OR he or she marked the answers in response to *the wrong questions,* then the game continues until there is a proper winner.

11. If you want to play again, reshuffle the cards and begin again.

Have fun!

TERMS

ABBREVIATIONS	MODIFY
ADJECTIVE	MOOD
ADVERB	NOUN
AGREEMENT	PARAGRAPH
ANTONYM	PARENTHESES
APOSTROPHE	PARTICIPLE
ARTICLE	PERIOD
CAPITALIZATION	PERSON
CASE	PHRASE
CLAUSE	PLURAL
COLON	PREDICATE
COMMA	PREFIX
CONJUNCTION	PREPOSITION
CONTRACTION	PRONOUN
DANGLING MODIFIER	PUNCTUATION
DASH (EM DASH)	ROOT
DECLARATIVE	SEMICOLON
ELLIPSIS	SENTENCE
EXCLAMATORY	SUBJECT
FRAGMENT	SUFFIX
GENDER	SYLLABLE
GERUND	SYNONYM
INFINITIVE	TENSE
INTERJECTION	VERB
INTERROGATIVE	VOICE

Additional Terms

Choose as many additional terms as you would like and write them in the squares. Repeat each as desired.
Cut out the squares and randomly distribute them to the class.
Instruct the students to place their square on the center space of their card.

Grammar and Usage Bingo

Clues for Additional Terms

Write three clues for each of your additional terms.

_____ 1. 2. 3.	_____ 1. 2. 3.
_____ 1. 2. 3.	_____ 1. 2. 3.
_____ 1. 2. 3.	_____ 1. 2. 3.

! ? . . , .	! ? . . , .	! ? . . , .	! ? . . , .	! ? . . , .
! ? . . , .	! ? . . , .	! ? . . , .	! ? . . , .	! ? . . , .
! ? . . , .	! ? . . , .	! ? . . , .	! ? . . , .	! ? . . , .
! ? . . , .	! ? . . , .	! ? . . , .	! ? . . , .	! ? . . , .
! ? . . , .	! ? . . , .	! ? . . , .	! ? . . , .	! ? . . , .
! ? . . , .	! ? . . , .	! ? . . , .	! ? . . , .	! ? . . , .
! ? . . , .	! ? . . , .	! ? . . , .	! ? . . , .	! ? . . , .

Abbreviations
1. They are the shortened forms of words.
2. Some ___ of common titles and positions of rank include Dr., Prof., Pres., Gov., and Adm.
3. We use lower-case letters and a period for most ___ of Latin terms. Examples are *i.e, e.g, et al., ca.,* and *vs.*

Adjective
1. Its main role is to modify, or limit, a noun or a pronoun.
2. The comparative form of this part of speech usually ends in *-er.* The superlative form of this part of speech usually ends in *-est.*
3. In the sentence "They are tired," the word *tired* is a predicate ___.

Adverb
1. An ___ can modify verbs, adjectives, clauses, sentences and other ___s, but it cannot modify a noun.
2. It often answers questions like how?, when?, where?, why? and to what extent?
3. A conjunctive ___ functions as a conjunction. Examples are *however, nevertheless,* and *therefore.*

Agreement
1. This term refers to the correspondence between words in gender, number, tense, case, and/or person.
2. Another word for this is *concord.*
3. The following sentence contains an error because there is a lack of ___ between the pronoun and its antecedent: "A person can get sick when they eat too much candy."

Antonym
1. It is the opposite of *synonym.*
2. It refers to a word in a pair of words that have opposite meanings.
3. *Hot* is an ___ of *cold. Brave* is an ___ of *cowardly.*

Apostrophe
1. This superscript sign is used to indicate the omission of one or more letters in a word.
2. This superscript sign is used to indicate possession.
3. This superscript sign is used to indicate the plural form of numbers, letters and abbreviations.

Article
1. There are two kinds of this part of speech: definite and indefinite.
2. The word *the* is a definite one.
3. The words *a* and *an* are indefinite ones.

Capitalization
1. It is the writing of a word with its first letter in upper case and the remaining letters in lower case.
2. According to the rules of ___, a sentence should begin with an upper-case letter.
2. According to the rules of ___, proper nouns are written with the first letter in upper case.

Case
1. A noun or pronoun that is the subject of a verb is said to be in the nominative ___.
2. A pronoun that is the object of a verb is said to be in the objective ___.
3. The possessive ___ is used to show ownership.

Clause
1. It is a group of words containing a subject and verb.
2. Although it has a subject and a verb, a subordinate, or dependent, one cannot stand alone as a sentence.
3. Unlike a subordinate one, an independent one can stand alone as a sentence.

Colon	Comma
1. This punctuation mark is sometimes used to introduce a series or a list.	1. Use a ___ to separate independent clauses joined by a coordinatingconjunction such as *and, but, for, or, nor, so,* or *yet.*
2. This punctuation mark is used after the salutation in a business letter.	2. This punctuation mark is used after introductory clauses.
3. This punctuation mark is used after a word introducing a quotation, explanation, example or series.	3. This punctuation mark is used to set off clauses, phrases, and words that are not essential to the meaning of the sentence.

Conjunction	Contraction
1. This part of speech connects two words, phrases or clauses.	1. It is the shortening of a word, syllable, or word group by omitting one or more letters and replacing them with an apostrophe.
2. Examples of coordinating ones are *and, but, for, or, nor, so,* and *yet.*	2. The word *won't* is a __ of the words *will not.*
3. A subordinating one introduces a subordinate clause and connects it with the main clause. Examples are *although, because* and, *until.*	3. The word *o'clock* is a ___ of the words *of the clock.*

Dangling Modifier	Dash (EM DASH)
1. It is a word, phrase or clause that does not connect grammatically with what it modifies.	1. Like a comma, it may be used to set off a parenthetical element in a sentence.
2. A ___ causes confusion because it modifies a word not clearly stated in the sentence.	2. Although it looks like a large hyphen, it does not function like one. Its function is similar to that of a parenthesis.
3. "While riding my bike, a squirrel crossed the street" is an example. It sounds like the squirrel was riding the bike!	3. A ___ is sometimes used to set off an appositive phrase that already includes commas.

Declarative	Ellipsis
1. This kind of sentence makes a statement.	1. This form of punctuation consists of 3 evenly spaced dots.
2. This kind of sentence does not give a command, make a request, exclaim, or ask a question.	2. This form of punctuation is used when omitting words from quoted material.
3. It is the most common type of sentence.	3. This form of punctuation is placed after the period when the omission comes at the end of a sentence; in that case there are four dots instead of three.

Exclamatory	Fragment
1. This type of sentence is actually a forceful form of a declaratory sentence.	1. This is an incomplete sentence.
2. This type of sentence shows strong feeling.	2. The second of the following sentences is an example: "Jack enjoys many genres of literature. Such as science fiction, historical fiction, and mysteries."
3. This kind of sentence ends with a special mark that consists of a vertical line above a dot.	3. "Walks the dog" is an example of this.

Grammar and Usage Bingo

Gender
1. Pronouns must agree in ___ and number with the nouns they replace. For example, we would say, "Rosa has her book" if it is Rosa's book.
2. Pronouns referring to people show ___ differentiation; those referring to objects do not.
3. Pronouns must agree in ___ with the nouns they replace. Female pronouns are *she* and *her.* Male pronouns are *he* and *him.*

Gerund
1. A ___ is a verb that ends in *-ing* and is used as a noun.
2. In the following sentence, the word *eating* is one: "I love eating ice cream on the porch."
3. "Reading a book " is an example of a ___ phrase.

Infinitive
1. It begins with the word *to* and is followed by the simple form of a verb.
2. It can be used as a noun, an adjective or an adverb. The following is an example of its use as a noun: "To practice is important."
3. An example is "to eat."

Interjection
1. It shows emotion and has no grammatical relationship to the rest of the sentence.
2. The following are examples of this type of word or phrase: *Wow, Hey,* and *Oh.*
3. It is a sudden, short utterance added to a sentence to show emotion. The following sentence contains an example: "Ouch, it stung me!"

Interrogative
1. This type of sentence asks a question.
2. This type of sentence ends with a question mark.
3. Many sentences of this type often begin with one of these words: *Who, When, What, Where, Why,* or *How.*

Modify
1. Adjectives and adverbs ___ other words. They make those words more specific.
2. An adjective can ___ a noun or a pronoun.
3. An adverb can ___ a verb, an adjective, or another adverb.

Mood
1. In the indicative ___ the verb states a fact or asks a question.
2. In the imperative ___ the verb gives a command or makes a request.
3. In the subjunctive ___ the verb expresses a desire, possibility or condition that is contrary to fact at the present time.

Noun
1. It is a word that names a person, animal, place, thing, or abstract idea.
2. A proper one names a specific person, place or thing and is capitalized.
3. A common one names something general and is not capitalized.

Paragraph
1. It is the fundamental unit of a composition.
2. It always begins on a new line and is often indented.
3. It deals with a main point or idea and this idea is supported by details.

Parentheses
1. It is a set of curved-bracket punctuation marks.
2. Like commas or dashes, these marks may be used to enclose a parenthetical expression.
3. These marks are always in a set of two.

Participle 1. This is a non-finite form of a verb; in other words, it cannot function on its own as the core of an independent sentence. 2. It is used to form compound tenses such as present, past and future progressive.; present, past and future perfect; and so on. 3. This non-finite form of the verb can be used as an adjective. An example is *smoked* bacon.	**Period** 1. This punctuation mark is used to end a declarative sentence. 2. This punctuation mark is used to end mild imperatives that do not require an exclamation point. 3. Some abbreviations end in this punctuation mark; others do not.
Person 1. This grammatical category is based on the relationship between the speaker and the listener or reader. 2. Some first-___ pronouns are *I, we, me, us, my, mine,* and *our.* 3. Some second-___ pronouns are *you* and *your.* Some third-___ pronouns are *he, she, it, they, him, her, them, his, hers* and *their.*	**Phrase** 1. It is a group of words that has no subject and/or no predicate but has a function in a sentence. 2. The following ___ has no subject: "is eating lunch." 3. The following ___ has no predicate: "the smiling children."
Plural 1. This form of most nouns is derived by adding "s" or "es" to the singular form. 2. To create this form of nouns ending in "y," drop the "y" and add "ies." 3. The ___ form of some nouns are irregular; some examples are *men, women* and *children.*	**Predicate** 1. It tells something about the subject of a complete sentence and always includes a verb. 2. Every complete sentence has a subject and a ___. 3. The following sentence has a compound one: "The playful dog **wagged** his tail and **licked** his owner's face."
Prefix 1. This affix is placed before the root to modify or change the meaning of the word. 2. An example is *circum-*, which means "around." It is found in the words *circumnavigate, circumstance, circumference,* and *circulatory.* 3. An example is *equi-*, which means "equal." It is found in the words *equilateral, equilibrium, equitable, equation,* and *equator.*	**Preposition** 1. This part of speech links nouns, pronouns and phrases to other words in the sentence. *Over, in, above, among, to* and *with* are examples 2. In the following sentence, the word *chalkboard* is the object a ___: "The teacher wrote the homework assignment **on the chalkboard.**" 3. In this sentence the word *to* is a ___: "The young boy walked **to** the principal's office."
Pronoun 1. This part of speech is used to refer to a noun or to another ___. 2. The noun or pronoun to which this part of speech refers is called the antecedent. 3. There are several types of this part of speech: personal *(he)*, relative *(who)*, indefinite *(each)*, demonstrative *(this)*, interrogative *(Who?)*, and reflexive *(myself)*.	**Punctuation** 1. It is the system inserting marks or signs in written material to clarify the meaning and to separate structural units. 2. The comma, the question mark, the colon, and the semi-colon are some ___ marks. 3. The ___ mark used to show surprise is an exclamation point.

Grammar and Usage Bingo

Root 1. It is the basic part of the word. It provides the basis from which a word is derived by adding affixes. 2. By adding prefixes and suffixes to the ___, we can get many different words. 3. *Cogn-* is the ___ of the words *recognize, cognitive,* and *incognito.*	**Semicolon** 1. We may use this punctuation mark to link two independent clauses without a connecting word. 2. We use this punctuation mark to link two independent clauses with a conjunctive adverb, such as *however, therefore,* or *nevertheless.* 3. We sometimes use this punctuation mark to separate items in a list if the items themselves contain commas.
Sentence 1. It is a group of words that communicate a complete thought. 2. Two independent clauses not properly connected result in a run-on ___. 3. A compound one consists of at least two independent clauses.	**Subject** 1. It is the word or word group about which something is said or written. 2. The ___ of a clause or sentence is always a noun or pronoun. 3. In the following sentence, the words *Jessica and her kitten* are the ___: "Jessica and her kitten sat on the couch together."
Suffix 1. This affix is placed after the root to modify or change the meaning of the word. 2. An example is *-logy,* which means "study of." It is found in the words *biology, ecology,* and *mythology.* 3. The ___ *-ly* can change an adjective into an adverb.	**Syllable** 1. It is a unit of spoken language larger than a phoneme. 2. It is word or part of a word that is sounded without interruption of the voice. 3. It consists of one or more vowel or syllabic consonant sounds alone or with consonant sounds before or after it.
Synonym 1. It refers to a word in a pair of words that have similar meanings. 2. It is the opposite of an *antonym.* 3. *Tepid* is a ___ of *warm. Vigilant* is a ___ of *watchful.*	**Tense** 1. The term comes from the Latin word *tempus,* which means "time." 2. The ___ of a verb indicates when an action or condition occurred; it may also show whether or not an action or condition was continuous or repetitive. 3. There are 14 ___ in English. The three basic ones are present, past, and future.
Verb 1. This part of speech expresses an action, an occurrence or a condition. 2. The three properties of this part of speech are tense, voice, and mood. 3. Linking ones are intransitive. Action ones may be transitive or intransitive; in other words, they may or may not have a direct object.	**Voice** 1. The ___ of a verb may be active or passive depending upon whether the action is done by the subject or to the subject. 2. The ___ of the verb in the following sentence is active: "Andrea kicked the ball." 3. The ___ of the verb in the following sentence is passive: "The ball was kicked by Andrea."

Grammar and Usage Bingo

© **Barbara M Peller**

Grammar & Usage Bingo

Preposition	Abbreviations	Adverb	Exclamatory	Antonym
Dash	Adjective	Tense	Parentheses	Root
Synonym	Modify		Plural	Verb
Syllable	Punctuation	Suffix	Paragraph	Period
Phrase	Gerund	Contraction	Sentence	Interrogative

Grammar & Usage Bingo

Syllable	Synonym	Interjection	Pronoun	Noun
Period	Declarative	Capitalization	Punctuation	Person
Clause	Gerund		Infinitive	Suffix
Predicate	Prefix	Modify	Voice	Antonym
Root	Tense	Contraction	Dash	Sentence

Grammar & Usage Bingo

Gerund	Suffix	Declarative	Paragraph	Synonym
Period	Adjective	Case	Abbreviations	Gender
Punctuation	Tense		Person	Agreement
Modify	Clause	Phrase	Predicate	Interjection
Sentence	Colon	Contraction	Voice	Noun

Grammar & Usage Bingo

Modify	Person	Adverb	Colon	Noun
Participle	Article	Abbreviations	Pronoun	Synonym
Plural	Predicate		Interrogative	Exclamatory
Suffix	Modify	Tense	Contraction	Capitalization
Comma	Root	Apostrophe	Sentence	Verb

© Barbara M Peller

Grammar & Usage Bingo

Root	Antonym	Punctuation	Capitalization	Colon
Participle	Suffix	Case	Infinitive	Adjective
Adverb	Verb		Parentheses	Fragment
Interrogative	Noun	Preposition	Voice	Conjunction
Declarative	Contraction	Synonym	Modify	Plural

© Barbara M Peller

Grammar & Usage Bingo

Agreement	Person	Declarative	Noun	Verb
Paragraph	Punctuation	Conjunction	Abbreviations	Synonym
Pronoun	Comma		Article	Infinitive
Contraction	Phrase	Voice	Apostrophe	Adverb
Period	Capitalization	Preposition	Plural	Dangling Modifier

Grammar & Usage Bingo

Preposition	Person	Fragment	Suffix	Declarative
Period	Noun	Gerund	Adjective	Participle
Interjection	Exclamatory		Infinitive	Article
Modify	Predicate	Case	Syllable	Clause
Contraction	Colon	Voice	Apostrophe	Agreement

© Barbara M Peller

Grammar & Usage Bingo

Plural	Person	Ellipsis	Paragraph	Article
Participle	Adverb	Pronoun	Verb	Capitalization
Dangling Modifier	Colon		Noun	Antonym
Sentence	Modify	Syllable	Comma	Predicate
Tense	Contraction	Apostrophe	Punctuation	Period

Grammar and Usage Bingo: Card No. 8

Grammar & Usage Bingo

Infinitive	Declarative	Gerund	Dangling Modifier	Colon
Comma	Noun	Plural	Punctuation	Person
Gender	Preposition		Adjective	Ellipsis
Conjunction	Antonym	Phrase	Parentheses	Fragment
Predicate	Voice	Case	Syllable	Interrogative

Grammar & Usage Bingo

Syllable	Paragraph	Article	Pronoun	Dangling Modifier
Verb	Capitalization	Abbreviations	Adjective	Noun
Colon	Person		Exclamatory	Clause
Phrase	Interrogative	Conjunction	Voice	Gender
Case	Period	Declarative	Root	Plural

Grammar & Usage Bingo

Agreement	Person	Punctuation	Conjunction	Period
Ellipsis	Gender	Parentheses	Infinitive	Abbreviations
Participle	Noun		Dash	Gerund
Case	Synonym	Voice	Colon	Syllable
Comma	Contraction	Preposition	Apostrophe	Declarative

© Barbara M Peller

Grammar & Usage Bingo

Declarative	Antonym	Gender	Paragraph	Infinitive
Gerund	Period	Adverb	Apostrophe	Adjective
Preposition	Fragment		Verb	Pronoun
Contraction	Predicate	Noun	Syllable	Participle
Person	Ellipsis	Colon	Comma	Capitalization

Grammar & Usage Bingo

Conjunction	Antonym	Agreement	Gender	Verb
Adverb	Ellipsis	Noun	Infinitive	Clause
Paragraph	Capitalization		Gerund	Fragment
Plural	Voice	Article	Colon	Syllable
Contraction	Interrogative	Apostrophe	Preposition	Parentheses

Grammar & Usage Bingo

Dash	Noun	Punctuation	Infinitive	Comma
Capitalization	Preposition	Gender	Adjective	Person
Conjunction	Exclamatory		Interjection	Case
Interrogative	Voice	Colon	Article	Agreement
Contraction	Pronoun	Clause	Period	Plural

Grammar & Usage Bingo

Parentheses	Infinitive	Punctuation	Declarative	Paragraph
Agreement	Dash	Abbreviations	Adverb	Comma
Verb	Preposition		Synonym	Person
Contraction	Gender	Ellipsis	Voice	Conjunction
Period	Predicate	Apostrophe	Dangling Modifier	Gerund

© Barbara M Peller

Grammar & Usage Bingo

Article	Gender	Ellipsis	Dangling Modifier	Prefix
Pronoun	Clause	Fragment	Participle	Exclamatory
Conjunction	Antonym		Verb	Gerund
Modify	Capitalization	Contraction	Parentheses	Syllable
Comma	Subject	Apostrophe	Predicate	Person

Grammar & Usage Bingo

Case	Semicolon	Mood	Gender	Dash
Parentheses	Comma	Voice	Exclamatory	Fragment
Infinitive	Plural		Subject	Ellipsis
Interrogative	Period	Syllable	Punctuation	Clause
Phrase	Conjunction	Declarative	Paragraph	Antonym

Grammar & Usage Bingo

Dangling Modifier	Colon	Capitalization	Conjunction	Pronoun
Person	Case	Phrase	Verb	Comma
Infinitive	Clause		Mood	Adverb
Antonym	Abbreviations	Voice	Syllable	Interjection
Subject	Gender	Punctuation	Semicolon	Agreement

Grammar & Usage Bingo

Verb	Agreement	Gender	Ellipsis	Syllable
Parentheses	Paragraph	Person	Declarative	Exclamatory
Semicolon	Colon		Adjective	Synonym
Interjection	Subject	Phrase	Predicate	Mood
Adverb	Prefix	Period	Plural	Apostrophe

© **Barbara M Peller**

Grammar & Usage Bingo

Dash	Semicolon	Paragraph	Gender	Apostrophe
Capitalization	Gerund	Participle	Phrase	Pronoun
Antonym	Fragment		Modify	Abbreviations
Root	Tense	Sentence	Predicate	Subject
Suffix	Plural	Prefix	Syllable	Mood

Grammar and Usage Bingo: Card No. 20

Grammar & Usage Bingo

Parentheses	Agreement	Participle	Gender	Root
Antonym	Mood	Article	Ellipsis	Preposition
Clause	Period		Semicolon	Punctuation
Phrase	Declarative	Subject	Interrogative	Plural
Modify	Prefix	Apostrophe	Case	Predicate

Grammar & Usage Bingo

Dangling Modifier	Interjection	Mood	Adverb	Conjunction
Pronoun	Paragraph	Synonym	Ellipsis	Adjective
Capitalization	Exclamatory		Preposition	Fragment
Subject	Interrogative	Predicate	Abbreviations	Participle
Prefix	Case	Semicolon	Clause	Interjection

Grammar & Usage Bingo

Article	Semicolon	Declarative	Adverb	Apostrophe
Agreement	Dash	Period	Parentheses	Abbreviations
Interjection	Conjunction		Sentence	Preposition
Clause	Prefix	Subject	Case	Predicate
Root	Tense	Plural	Phrase	Mood

Grammar & Usage Bingo

Article	Plural	Dash	Semicolon	Ellipsis
Mood	Apostrophe	Participle	Pronoun	Preposition
Fragment	Dangling Modifier		Conjunction	Clause
Root	Sentence	Subject	Case	Antonym
Suffix	Modify	Prefix	Paragraph	Tense

Grammar & Usage Bingo

Modify	Participle	Semicolon	Punctuation	Mood
Abbreviations	Antonym	Parentheses	Article	Adjective
Interrogative	Ellipsis		Sentence	Subject
Synonym	Root	Tense	Prefix	Exclamatory
Apostrophe	Dash	Capitalization	Comma	Suffix

Grammar & Usage Bingo

Mood	Semicolon	Interjection	Pronoun	Dangling Modifier
Phrase	Paragraph	Ellipsis	Dash	Article
Interrogative	Sentence		Exclamatory	Modify
Case	Adverb	Root	Prefix	Subject
Fragment	Comma	Punctuation	Tense	Suffix

Grammar and Usage Bingo: Card No. 26

Grammar & Usage Bingo

Interjection	Capitalization	Semicolon	Dash	Gerund
Root	Sentence	Parentheses	Subject	Adjective
Voice	Tense		Prefix	Modify
Dangling Modifier	Agreement	Participle	Suffix	Abbreviations
Comma	Exclamatory	Mood	Synonym	Fragment

Grammar and Usage Bingo: Card No. 27

Grammar & Usage Bingo

Interjection	Dash	Synonym	Semicolon	Article
Gerund	Mood	Sentence	Pronoun	Exclamatory
Tense	Clause		Fragment	Phrase
Syllable	Dangling Modifier	Period	Prefix	Subject
Adverb	Infinitive	Comma	Suffix	Root

Grammar & Usage Bingo

Mood	Dash	Dangling Modifier	Parentheses	Infinitive
Predicate	Phrase	Participle	Fragment	Synonym
Interrogative	Sentence		Adjective	Semicolon
Gerund	Root	Noun	Prefix	Subject
Article	Ellipsis	Suffix	Agreement	Tense

Grammar & Usage Bingo

Colon	Semicolon	Pronoun	Infinitive	Subject
Abbreviations	Dash	Declarative	Exclamatory	Adjective
Interrogative	Conjunction		Fragment	Participle
Suffix	Agreement	Adverb	Prefix	Sentence
Root	Verb	Tense	Mood	Synonym

www.ingramcontent.com/pod-product-compliance
Lightning Source LLC
LaVergne TN
LVHW061341060426
835511LV00014B/2049